FORGIVE YOURSELF FIRST

FORGIVE YOURSELF FIRST
A Guide To Personal Peace

Velma Callan Harland

BALBOA
PRESS
A DIVISION OF HAY HOUSE

Copyright © 2012 Velma Callan Harland.

All rights reserved. No part of this book may be used or reproduced by any means, graphic, electronic, or mechanical, including photocopying, recording, taping or by any information storage retrieval system without the written permission of the publisher except in the case of brief quotations embodied in critical articles and reviews.

Editor: Final Copy Editorial Services

Balboa Press books may be ordered through booksellers or by contacting:

Balboa Press
A Division of Hay House
1663 Liberty Drive
Bloomington, IN 47403
www.balboapress.com
1-(877) 407-4847

ISBN: 978-1-4525-4574-5 (sc)
ISBN: 978-1-4525-4576-9 (hc)
ISBN: 978-1-4525-4575-2 (e)

Library of Congress Control Number: 2012900785

Because of the dynamic nature of the Internet, any web addresses or links contained in this book may have changed since publication and may no longer be valid. The views expressed in this work are solely those of the author and do not necessarily reflect the views of the publisher, and the publisher hereby disclaims any responsibility for them.

The author of this book does not dispense medical advice or prescribe the use of any technique as a form of treatment for physical, emotional, or medical problems without the advice of a physician, either directly or indirectly. The intent of the author is only to offer information of a general nature to help you in your quest for emotional and spiritual well-being. In the event you use any of the information in this book for yourself, which is your constitutional right, the author and the publisher assume no responsibility for your actions.

Certain stock imagery © Thinkstock.
Any people depicted in stock imagery provided by Thinkstock are models, and such images are being used for illustrative purposes only.

Printed in the United States of America

Balboa Press rev. date: 6/5/2012

*This guidebook is dedicated to my family.
I am so grateful for every one of you.
Thank you for the lessons.*

Self-forgiveness is giving up all hope for a better past.
—bumper sticker

Contents

Acknowledgments ix
Introduction. xi
1. Are You Willing to Forgive Yourself?. 1
2. Are You Willing to Change Yourself? 15
3. Releasing Guilt and Shame 27
4. Identifying Defense Mechanisms, Anger, and Resentment. . . 37
5. Seeing Things Differently 49
6. Prayer and Meditation. 63
7. Getting There—Formulating a Plan and
   Putting It All Together. 71
8. Learn to Relax. 79
Sources and Related Reading 93
About the Author 95

Acknowledgments

Throughout this guidebook, I share many stories about people's lives, which I hope will inspire readers to begin their own journeys of self-forgiveness. All of these stories are true, though names have been changed and identities disguised. I want to acknowledge, with much appreciation, the people behind these stories.

I also want to acknowledge the support and encouragement of some special friends and colleagues. I am especially grateful for the unexpected, gentle prodding that would arrive from one of you by mail, telephone, or e-mail at exactly those times when I wanted to stop writing. Thank you so much, Susan, Katey, Lois, Peter, Veronica, Anne, Sharon, Kay, Jim, and Kathy. This book could never have been written without you.

And, of course, special acknowledgement goes to my husband, Harv, who has been terrific and even prepared a few meals when I was too absorbed in my task to part with it, even for nourishment. Harv also supported me by reading the manuscript and giving me feedback and encouragement.

Finally, I want to acknowledge with gratitude all outside sources quoted or otherwise used in this book and to offer my sincere apologies where full and proper attribution may be lacking.

Again, thank you, one and all.

Velma Harland

Introduction

Forgive Yourself First takes you on a journey to a better place. Along the way, you will gather a number of practical skills to help you see and deal with life situations differently. These new tools will enable you, when necessary, to choose a better path forward than you might have chosen in the past.

To begin, we examine just what self-forgiveness really means. You will look at your own life story, the one that brought you to this book, and examine your established behavioral patterns, your emotions, and the role your ego has played in your life.

A word of caution: as you progress in this journey, you might come to face the real you for the first time. Fear not, however; you will also learn strategies that will help move you to the next stop on the trip. You will learn how to identify and face your feelings and emotions, including guilt, shame, anger, and resentment, and to recognize some of the most common defenses people use against these fearful demons. What defenses do you use?

Near the journey's end, you will learn to better recognize your established patterns of behavior and begin to understand their consequences. How have specific events from your past influenced your present challenges? How do your current beliefs cause your reactions to life situations?

People can evolve spiritually by examining what they like and dislike in the actions of other people and understanding why. But then what? It is important to know the difference between making amends and apologizing.

Finally, you will learn how to maintain peace in any situation. To this end, humor and relaxation techniques are introduced, along with the role of prayer and meditation. These practices are important because attitude always precedes behavior, as does your level of contentedness with life.

Finally, the book guides you through a review of the tools you have collected on this journey and placed in your personal toolbox and then helps you formulate a plan for going forward.

1
Are You Willing to Forgive Yourself?

Trembling with anxiety and crying uncontrollably, Maureen sat with her head in her hands. She was living a nightmare and couldn't wake herself up. She felt sick to her stomach as she relived, over and over, the nightmare trip to the shopping center.

It was the first day back to school after the summer holiday. Maureen and her four children were excited as they jumped into the car, the children with their respective lists of school supplies clenched tightly in their fists. All the way to the mall, they talked incessantly about what was on those lists and what kind of this or color of that they were going to get.

Shopping with all four was an all-consuming task for Maureen, but finally it was done, and they piled back into the car with their bags of pens, pencils, books, and scribblers. They were pulling out of the parking lot, everyone happy and chattering all at the same time, when Maureen's cell phone rang. As she fumbled around for it while trying to navigate the turn onto the busy street, she heard a sickening thud and instinctively slammed on the brakes.

The children screamed in horror as a young motorcycle driver flew through the air in front of their vehicle, landing several feet away on the center of the boulevard . . . motionless.

Instantly, people were running around everywhere. Maureen virtually flew to the leather-clad man in the middle of the street. After what seemed like an eternity, an ambulance arrived and took the young man to the hospital. Someone had called 911. She didn't know whom, but she knew it wasn't her, and she felt bad about that.

Maureen wanted to follow the ambulance to be sure he was all right, but with the children, and then the police officers wanting to talk to her, she could not. Finally, over an hour later, she was told she could take her children home, but she shook so much and was so distraught she could scarcely remember how to drive.

Back home at last, she immediately called her husband, Sam, and through her tears asked him to come home from work. Sam arrived just in time to receive the news that Jonathan, the young motorcyclist, had broken his left leg, but he was recovering nicely.

* * *

While they may not be as dramatic, or traumatic, as Maureen's, everyone has experiences that call for forgiveness, primarily of oneself, before one can move forward. I believe it's impossible to make progress toward peace until you learn to forgive yourself. Self-forgiveness clears out the mental and emotional confusion that can cause a great deal of anxiety and wasted time in your life.

Unfortunately, people tend to rerun their mistakes over and over in their minds, adding more self-criticism every time they do so.

As much as I would like to be perfect all the time, I accept that it is never going to happen. If I refuse to forgive myself, I will likely spend much of my life in the past, rather than in the present. Yet, is not the present all any of us really ever has?

In order to experience spiritual peace, self-forgiveness is necessary, but most of us don't really know what it is or how to go about achieving it. In my experience, the first step is to conquer the fear of making more mistakes, because that fear will stop you dead in your tracks when it comes to setting and achieving new goals, leaving you stuck in the ruts of your own muddy road.

Moving forward with self-forgiveness is difficult, if not impossible, as long as fear is your constant companion. We have to accept that we are human beings, which means we are both perfect and imperfect—the essence of the human experience.

A bumper sticker I once saw put it most succinctly:
Self-forgiveness is giving up all hope for a better past.
In reality, it is composed of many things:

- accepting yourself as a person who has faults and makes mistakes
- letting go of self-blame and anger over past failures
- calling an end to beating yourself up for past mistakes
- putting down the tremendous burden of guilt
- calling an end to obsessively thinking about past mistakes and failures
- giving up all forms of punishing, self-destructive behavior
- becoming willing to forgive others for their mistakes and failures
- becoming aware of your low self-esteem and giving up resistance to doing what is necessary to improve it
- facing and accepting what is

Perpetually beating yourselves up over past mistakes is to live with the assumption that you already had all the knowledge and experience you needed to avoid those mistakes and make better decisions, and that, often, is just not the case. Despite this, once a mistake has been made and regret sets in, you feel you deserve to be punished because you think you are unworthy and undeserving.

Like Maureen, you might ask yourself, "How can I live with myself after having done such a thing to another human being?"

So, you must first decide if you are, in fact, willing to forgive yourself, to let go of the habit of feeling shameful and guilty. Perhaps you are just not ready to forgive yourself for not knowing everything you needed to know at the time of the so-called mistake or failure.

Ask yourself, what would you have needed to know in order to have acted differently? In fact, take a few minutes to ponder this question, and write down what comes to mind.

Am I willing to forgive myself for not being wiser and more aware? If not, why not? What did I need to know in order to have acted differently?

_____
_____
_____
_____
_____
_____
_____
_____
_____
_____
_____

I think the responsible, logical conclusion we must all finally come to in this process, if we are honest with ourselves, is that we did the best we could with the information we had at the time we "failed" or made that dreadful "mistake." But even if you are tempted to come to a different conclusion, I personally have never found that beating myself up ever changed the past. What works much better is to take a step back and objectively try to figure out what actually went wrong and then move forward.

If you can be wise enough and brave enough to look at your mistakes and discover what went wrong in the past, you are on the road to a better future. It's almost trite to say it, but every mistake does contain a lesson—look for it!

It is logical to assume that if you can acknowledge that you did the best you could at the time with the knowledge and awareness that you had, then you are taking blame out of the picture, which makes it much easier to move on from the experience with something more worthwhile, such as self-honesty.

If it is causing pain, your current way of dealing with past events has not been working well for you, so it is fundamental to accept that you need to change your thinking and behavior patterns if you want an end to that pain. If you don't learn to forgive yourself, you will miss an opportunity to transform your pain into an experience that can help you grow.

Imagine your past as a compost heap that contains all the rotten experiences you want to get rid of—all the pain and all the suffering. Like a real compost heap, if you stir it up every so often, it eventually transforms into wonderful, life-supporting humus. Begin the process of letting the past turn into something positive.

This is not a new concept, by the way. People often extract a lot of good from the experience of some pretty serious pain in their lives: consider Mothers Against Drunk Drivers and twelve-step groups, for example. Mental and emotional waste can, indeed, be transformed into the wonderful humus of spirituality.

Self-forgiveness is neither a simple nor a one-time event. It is always a work in progress. Like a seed growing into a flower, it takes time. And just when you think you have it well in hand, you might find other issues surfacing that you didn't even know were there, issues that also need attention—such as the need to forgive.

I don't think anyone ever masters self-forgiveness completely, but I do think we can acquire the skills needed to better handle whatever comes our way. It is also important to realize that many of us who think we can't let go of the past have simply learned not to let go. Perhaps there were times in your life when hurtful things were said that injured you so deeply that the notion of "letting it go" is abhorrent to you. Maybe things were not said that needed to be said. Things that were done, or not done, might have hurt you and, taken together, they have shaped and defined who you are today. It's only logical that changing the effects of years of accumulated experience can be a significant challenge.

Many of us have valued confidants: spouses, friends, and professional counselors. These well-meaning people tell us, "Just let it go." And we invariably reply, "How?"

But consider the cost of not letting go. I was at a workshop once when the instructor said, "Clench your fist, and raise your arm in the air. Now, continuing to keep your fist clenched, hold that position for thirty minutes."

It didn't take long to understand just how much energy it takes to hold onto anything—mental energy, emotional energy, physical energy, and spiritual energy. I realized that day that I wanted to use my energy in the best possible, most productive manner and not waste it by "holding on."

In my role as a yoga teacher for many years, I have witnessed students physically and emotionally let go as they enter deeply into an asana (yoga posture) and let themselves be in the present moment. That is what we all need to do. Make a decision to unlearn the bad habit of hanging onto all your past hurts and mistakes.

In my forgiveness work, I have often heard people say, "It is so much harder to forgive yourself than it is to forgive another person." You realize that forgiving others is a desirable thing to do, but how do you forgive yourself? Well, consider that maybe it will actually be easier to forgive yourself than to forgive others because in forgiving yourself, you don't have to think about how the other person will react.

For example, my friend Roberta told me the story of her two aunts who were having some trouble with each other. Her Aunt Mary came to Roberta with a request for help in preparing to talk to her Aunt Annie for the purpose of initiating a reconciliation. Roberta and her Aunt Mary worked out what Mary wanted to say and they did some roll playing to get it right. Mary was sincere in wanting to resolve the difficulties between her sister Annie and herself. She had also made the decision to forgive herself before she approached Annie.

The whole issue had to do with the fact they believed the other had been saying unkind things about them and their families. They both felt betrayed. When Mary approached Annie to ask if they could clear the air, Annie said no. She told Mary what had taken place was far too hurtful for her. Annie began defending herself and then suddenly withdrew from the conversation.

Mary was a little surprised, but then reminded herself not to be attached to the outcome of her attempt to reconcile with Annie. After all, she only had the power to put down her own heavy load of guilt. She had no control over whether Annie would do the same.

So, with a great deal of grace, Mary made the decision to forgive Annie completely, regardless of what Annie's reaction might be. She silently blessed her, released her with love, and moved into a place of compassion for both of them. She knew that she had made the attempt to clear the air with Annie honestly. She had done everything she could.

Mary's desire to forgive suggested she was advanced in spiritual understanding and had determined to change her behavior toward Annie. It was important for Mary not to have any expectations about how her apology would be received so that her own self forgiveness would not hinge on Annie's willingness to reciprocate.

Forgiving is a slow and gradual process, which begins only when we *want* to forgive. That desire is the real beginning; it enables us to start changing how we think about the situation. Annie wasn't ready to forgive, and that is her own journey to deal with.

The Role of the Ego

I have found that at those times when my life was not working and I was in pain, my ego was very busy putting bandages over the wounds, layer after layer, burying them deeper and deeper, making them bigger and bigger, like my own private pearls.

When a foreign object, such as sand, gets into an oyster, the oyster starts coating the irritant with layers of a substance called nacre. The longer the irritant stays in the pearl, the more layers of nacre form. This process takes place to ensure the oyster doesn't suffer or feel pain.

In the same way, the ego thinks if it hides its undesirable feelings, its flaws and imperfections, its insecurities, mistakes, shame, and wounds deep enough, no one will ever discover the ugly truth—not even the ego itself—and it will be safe.

Suppose someone told you not to sing out loud in a choir but rather to just move your lips, or suppose someone told you that you are not smart enough. Any incident in which we are made to feel "less than" combines with similar incidents until the weight of it all becomes too much to bear.

Debbie Ford's book, *Why Good People Do Bad Things*, gives a good explanation of the ego, which is essential to understand. The ego is responsible in part for your survival, according to Ford. In order to function properly, the ego needs to be balanced. If your ego gets damaged, which can happen in so many ways in the normal course of everyday life, it becomes split, a wounded ego. It then needs tender loving care to come back into harmony as a completely healthy ego.

Suppose you have done all the study and preparation necessary for a particular career, which would be the healthy ego at work. Finally, you begin climbing the ladder in your chosen field. However, you start to become anxious as you realize just how many other people are trying to climb the same ladder. You become fearful that you may, indeed, not be smart enough or have what it takes to succeed in getting to the top. In this process, your ego becomes wounded, and a wounded ego thrives on competition as it strives to survive. Unfortunately, the competitive process can cause you to make more and more choices out of fear.

For example, you might become involved with someone who has a very bad reputation because you think the person might be helpful in some way to your climb up the ladder. You might pass someone else's project or ideas off as your own. Perhaps you tell some half-truths in order to look better in your boss's eyes. At some point, you begin to feel bad about your behavior, but you quiet the doubts and the little voice that asks, "Are you sure this is okay?"

After months or even years of this kind of behavior, the doubts become deeply buried. Remember the pearl? In time, after layer upon layer of nacre, a pearl can become very large and shiny. So, to carry the analogy to its logical conclusion, covering your wounds with bandages and admiring your ability to keep them hidden can lead to a very large ego and some extreme attitudes, such as the following:

- I am the richest.
- I am the thinnest.
- I am the greatest.

Or, conversely, and particularly for those of us who are oppressed by the constant effort to keep our wounds hidden, you might have the following attitudes:

- I am worthless.
- No one loves me.
- I am so stupid.

Now and again, you may want to make a choice from your better self, but eventually your wounded ego will have done so much internal damage that the negative voice will be the only one heard:

- I can't trust anyone.
- I have been hurt before, and I'm not taking any more chances.
- Nobody knows the pain I've endured.
- They're a bunch of idiots, and I don't need to listen to them.

When the ego is wounded, it refuses to see or hear any truth other than the one it tells itself. For the wounded ego to survive, it must be right about the way it sees itself, others, and the world at large. It manufactures circumstances that are consistent with the way it sees the world. I believe it is this wounded ego that is responsible for what has been called the biggest addiction in the world—the need to be right.

The unhealthy ego believes it must be right about everything, even if being right brings unwanted results, hurts others in the process, and leads to our becoming disengaged from ourselves.

The wounded ego truly believes that it can act in accordance with its own laws and get away with it. It tells itself,

- I am bigger and better; the rules don't apply to me.
- I can do what I want, and no one will find out.
- No one can tell me what to do.

When we are trying to outrun our shame, we may try various ways to make ourselves feel better, such as flirting and trying to seduce others who already have partners, in an effort to get the attention we feel we deserve.

Some egos believe the cure for their wounds is money, even if they have to resort to cheating, robbing, or embezzling to get it. Some people might even resort to all of these maneuvers to find ways to cover up negative emotions and inner turmoil.

When the bandages you have been putting over your wounds are no longer helping, and you are in so much pain that your life isn't working at all, you find yourself struggling with an ego that is falling apart. Fortunately, although this experience is fraught with many emotions—as the outer layer of the pearl is scraped away—it can be a positive turning point, a period of spiritual growth.

This is a period of healing that takes longer for some than others, because some people don't have just one pearl but a system of them.

In fact, some of us discover that we have whole strings of pearls. The healing will take even longer if you are resistant to being open and honest with yourself. But, ultimately, that's okay, because in this work, there is absolutely no rush.

Eckhart Tolle, spiritual teacher and author, tells us that the ego lives in the past and in the future but avoids the present. If we can be in the present moment and just observe our thoughts—become more detached from our thoughts than we used to be—then we will realize that self-descriptive words are only thoughts. For instance if you keep thinking I come from the wrong part of town therefore I must be useless. They are not who we really are!

My sincere belief is that by using the tools outlined in this book, you will be rewarded with greater understanding of what it is to live in peace as well as greater knowledge of your beliefs, values, attitudes, thoughts, and patterns of behavior.

Most importantly, you will come to understand what you want to change, and you will learn more effective ways to avoid sabotaging yourself.

The next step is to make a commitment to yourself by writing a "peace treaty" with yourself. The following is an example that will give you some ideas, but everyone's will be slightly different.

Peace Treaty

- I believe in the possibility of my spiritual growth.
- I promise to forgive myself for all the mistakes I have made.
- I promise to work on my self-esteem issues.
- I promise to stop beating myself up with destructive self-talk.

_____   _____
   Your name   Date

Now, complete the following statements as they apply to whatever it is you are blaming yourself for:

This wouldn't have happened if only I had . . .
___

This wouldn't have happened if only I hadn't . . .
___

What are some of your "if onlys"?
___

Has the inability to forgive yourself affected your emotional stability? If so, how?

_____
_____
_____
_____
_____
_____
_____
_____
_____

2

Are You Willing to Change Yourself?

It is now time to set out on our road trip. We are equipped with enough tools to enable us to keep going when we encounter speed bumps, detours, and roadblocks. We will take our time and enjoy this sacred life journey of self-forgiveness. Later, you will likely want to revisit some of the stops along the way.

The first tool you will need to take out of your spiritual toolbox is hope—hope that you will be creating a brighter future for yourself by the time this trip is done. Hope means opening yourself up to the possibility that you can change and accept help from others.

Hope is one of our internal tools, but we also need to recognize that there are many resources beyond ourselves that we can access, including a far greater power than ourselves.

Another great tool you can make use of every day is the practice of writing things down. You will be asked throughout this guidebook to use this tool, so you might want to dedicate a special journal to this self-forgiveness journey.

A friend once wrote to tell me he had just joined Overeaters Anonymous and that one of the things he really liked about the program was the practice of writing. Jack said they had taught him that when he wasn't sure what was bothering him or how to deal with it, he should take out a paper and pen and put down in black and white whatever he could about what was on his mind and how it made him feel.

Write until your pencil begins to tell you what is really going on inside your head. This is called stream-of-consciousness writing, and it can be for your eyes only.

Even if you know what is bothering you before you start, writing can be a good way of getting rid of it. The very act of putting your feelings onto paper helps to dissipate anger, fear, resentment, or self-pity. When you look at what you have written, you might see your previously overwhelming emotional reaction shrink to a manageable level.

I personally resisted journaling for some time, but I am now a total convert. It is one of the most effective ways of uncovering hidden emotions and can put you in touch with the flow and experience of your life. Jack's letter inspired me. I thought what he had learned sounded really helpful, so I decided I would try it.

Coincidentally, shortly after Jack's letter, I came across Julie Cameron's book, *The Artist's Way*, in which she writes about morning pages. (Cameron 1;5)

> I do not start a day without them. What exactly are morning pages? They sound like work. Why should we do them? They are three pages of daily longhand stream of consciousness, written first thing upon arising. An excellent meditation practice for hyperactive Westerners, the pages clarify and prioritize our day. Morning pages are not intended to be high art. They are not real writing. They are simply siphoning off of the mind's surface so that we can get to deeper thoughts and impulses.
>
> Morning pages leave no corner of our life unexamined. Our dreams, our hopes, our disappointments, our pains—all of these are grist for the mill. A day at a time, a page at a time, an issue at a time, we become intimate with ourselves. Our hidden feelings become known to us. (Cameron 1;5)

I love my morning pages, and I use them as a form of prayer. I start my pages every morning with "Dear God," and I wouldn't dream of missing them.

[1]Julie Cameron also tells us about Sister Raymond Mary, a nun who says, "I think of the pages as a meditation practice." She has been writing the pages for a decade, and they have apparently seen her through many shifting phases in her vocation. (Cameron 9)

"They are with me when I am full of faith and when I am full of doubt," she reports. "Their consistency gives me optimism. Optimism is a frequently reported fruit of morning pages. So is hope. As we take our hand to the page, we take our hand to our life. We are not victims, abandoned by a capricious deity to fend for ourselves. There is, we come to sense, a benevolent Something that receives what we write and acts upon it. Our clarity seems to trigger charity on our behalf."

Melody Beattie, in *Codependents' Guide to the Twelve Steps*, takes this approach to uncovering anger and other emotions. Beattie suggests that we take whatever is bothering us the most, whatever we feel we need self-forgiveness for, whatever is blocking us in a particular area, and sit down and write about it.

I have come to believe that the more we can write about ourselves, our feelings, and our beliefs, the more helpful writing will be for our work toward self-forgiveness. You need to be clear about what you want to forgive yourself for, of course, because you are taking the courageous step of bringing all aspects of yourself out into the light.

It has been said that 5 percent of people think on paper. The other 95 percent think over coffee. The most successful people are those who write things down.

So the first of a number of stops on our trip is not a rest stop but a "work stop," where you will write your personal story. If you don't know what your story is, ask yourself what brought you to this guidebook in the first place.

---

[1] *The Artist Way Workbook*

As you begin to write, remember that this is not a time to censor yourself; give yourself permission to write whatever comes to mind, including your deepest feelings.

My story is . . .

Finished? You will need your story later, but for now, put it aside.

The next step is to imagine your inner self as your personal house, and you are about to do some housework. Get your spiritual lantern and shine it into every corner of your house, and be prepared, with mop and pail, vacuum cleaner, and dusters, to clean out every room. No doubt you may well find several dark and closed-off rooms that have never been lived in.

You may also find rooms that are full of all kinds of things you didn't want, things on which you tried to force the door shut. Trying to keep that door shut has taken a lot of energy. Like a beach ball held underwater, the door will eventually pop out and hit you in the face.

As you clean, open the windows and let in some light. Dust away the cobwebs, but beware! As you go from room to room, you will likely experience some of the old emotions you have kept hidden, even from yourself. Unacknowledged emotions have probably led you into behavior patterns that may be a mystery even to you. Uncovering these hidden behavior patterns and associated emotions may take some time. It is best if you don't try to rush this important work.

In fact, you may find you need to ask a guide to help you—a trusted friend, relative, or counselor—someone with whom you feel completely comfortable.

Jane is in her late fifties. She blames her husband, Larry, for all her failures and unhappiness and enjoys playing the long-suffering martyr, basking in the sympathy of relatives. She has done this for a long time but has been unaware that she does it—not only with her husband but also with her children and even her grandchildren.

"If it weren't for Larry's inability to make enough money for the family to live comfortably," she whines to anyone who will listen, "everything would be perfect."

Larry is an electrician, and it is true that he can't seem to get and keep the big jobs. When he does make money, it disappears almost immediately.

Jane has always had a huge need to keep up with the Joneses, not understanding that this comes from a habit of looking for happiness outside of herself, or operating from her "ego state." I believe that whenever we are not at peace, we are being dominated by our egos, also known as our "lower selves."

One of Jane's associated habits has been to nag constantly, monitoring and trying to control every move members of her family make. The children feel as if they can't breathe, suffocated by her unrelenting control and constant demands.

One day, Jane discovered that Larry had been having an affair. It had ended, but the revelation served as a wake-up call for Jane. It was only then that she sought professional help. With the guidance of a counselor, she began the work of looking at her behaviors and gradually became aware of the way she tried to control everyone in her life. By not allowing others to be themselves, she had been trying to create dependency on her so that the relationships in her life would stay the way she wanted them, which made her feel safe.

Jane began to understand that she was going to continue to suffer if she kept expecting everyone else to behave the way she wanted them to. She started to see that she could still hope for the outcome she wanted, but she could also try to accept others for who they were.

Because it was part of Jane's approach to life to be a constant worrier, Jane's counselor pointed out to her that the work she was doing in uncovering her hidden emotions could be compared to the transformation of a caterpillar into a butterfly. The caterpillar does not know that it is going to be a butterfly. Each part of its death and rebirth in the cocoon has to be experienced.

A man once noticed a cocoon on a bush in his yard. As he started to remove it from the bush and throw it away, he noticed the end was opening and a butterfly was struggling to escape. In an effort to help the emerging butterfly, he carefully cut the cocoon away with a razor blade. The butterfly feebly crawled away from the open cocoon and, within a few hours, died.

Though the man had acted from good intentions, the butterfly had needed the strength it would have gained from the struggle to free itself in order to survive in the outside world.

Only we can find the answers for our own lives; only we can change our patterns of behavior, once we become aware of them. Any attempt by another person to do any of this work for us only limits our ability to grow and become strong.

Jane finally came to recognize how much damage she was doing to her children with her unrelenting control and constant worry. She hadn't realized that the more she worried, especially about her family, the more they picked up on that energy, which made them feel even more inadequate. Jane had heard the saying, "If you worry on their behalf, you are pouring gasoline on their fire." This time she really got the message.

In the early days of Jane's marriage to Larry, Jane's parents had given her a large amount of money. She insisted that Larry take the money so he could start his own business. This was completely her idea, yet when the business failed, she was consumed with resentment.

Her counselor helped her see that she was not only angry with Larry for his poor management of the money but also with herself for having given it away, because that meant she had given away her power as well. She began to understand that she had taken on the victim role by not being willing to take responsibility for her own life.

Overly critical and controlling patterns of behavior usually mean we are avoiding taking a good, hard look at ourselves.

Jane was shocked to realize that her loved ones were constantly defending their thinking, their friends, their behavior, and their lives while in her "courtroom." It was a revelation to her that she was thinking of herself as the all-powerful one, the one with all the answers, and she decided to make a new policy. She was going to let others—even her children—live their own lives.

Jane stopped confusing her obligations as a parent with an attitude that put unrealistic expectations on other people. She became aware that she had a right to live her own life, and she began trying to allow others the same right. She made the decision that whenever her loved ones weren't doing what she wanted them to do, she was going to forgive them.

This is such a common phenomenon, especially among parents with whom I have worked. They take on extra responsibility for others and, in the process, become anxious, fearful, and develop feelings of low self-worth, anger, and resentment. They sometimes need a complete overhaul of their thinking.

When they are relating their stories to me, I tell these people that they can rip out their hearts and offer them to the children they are so worried about, and their children's bodies will likely reject the transplant. They will not have done their children any good, and they most certainly will have destroyed themselves in the process.

As she continued on her journey, Jane gradually began to develop a willingness to stand back and allow those she loved to grow in whatever ways they needed to grow. She did not find it easy to let the people around her lead their own lives, but she knew she had to and that it was necessary that she change her behavior patterns.

In the end, as Jane continued to focus her attention on her emotions, she understood how she was reacting to pain. She saw how she was holding onto it. She began to realize that, despite any other person's role in creating the situation, she was responsible for what she did with her pain. Self-forgiveness is about accepting responsibility for your emotional reactions. You need to let pain go, and trust is an essential element of letting go.

I recently heard that the twelve-step movement would probably be considered the most important spiritual movement in the twentieth century. This is because it is based on surrender. People who are in recovery programs know that they can't do it all by themselves. When they start trying to control everything, they usually fail; they need to surrender.

Just like people with addictions, we seem to have to hit bottom, to be at our weakest and most vulnerable, before we finally admit that our lives aren't working well and that we must seek help. That is when we are most open to God's grace. But what is God's grace? The best explanation I have heard is that it is an unearned gift, the loving movement of God in our lives.

Everyone needs to ask herself what the things are she needs to let go of, such as old wounds. Unfortunately, you can't let go of something until you know what it is, until you have spent some time with your pain. Sooner or later, we all need to stop rehashing in our minds, stop holding grudges and carrying on a war. We need to stop feeling self-pity, apathy, and anger. We need to let go, because the old emotions and wounded memories will steal life away. Most importantly, we will not find peace and bring joy and happiness into our lives until we are willing to let go.

So, ask yourself the following questions:

1. Can I let go of trying to be accepted for what I do and look to being accepted for who I am?
2. Can I let go of my anxiety?
3. Can I let go of my expectations of other people?
4. Can I let go of worry?
5. Can I let go of what others think of me?

If you find it difficult to let go (and it can take a long, long time), ask yourself if you are at least *willing* to let go. If the answer is yes, then ask yourself the critical question. When?

We all need to let go in order to find peace. The way we let go is to trust our lives to something greater than ourselves—to God. That means we need to surrender, which is a huge act of faith, and begin to live in the present moment.

Along the way, some of us stumble and struggle with the concept of God. We all have slightly different ideas about Him as a result of what we have been taught and been through in our lives. If we stay open, eventually most of us find our own paths to spirituality. Things seem to work out if we begin with whatever amount of belief, or disbelief, we possess and are open to growing from there.

Many of us grew up oriented to achievement and self-sufficiency rather than this idea of surrendering and putting our trust in something outside of ourselves. Admitting you need new attitudes and a way to self-forgiveness is the beginning of living in humility.

But who wants to be humble? The word itself may sound unappealing and old-fashioned, but to me it simply means being teachable. Humility makes us open to really listening to others and ourselves. It allows us to be open to *not* knowing and *not* being attached to outcomes that we are accustomed to clinging to for a sense of security.

You don't have to wear sackcloth and ashes to be humble, and you don't have to feel inferior. Being humble means having a realistic view of yourself that allows you to grow and not be locked into self-destructive patterns of behavior.

How many times have you tried to bluff your way through something because you were too embarrassed to admit that you didn't know? Change is much easier if you are not rigid with pride. If you are humble, you will not be afraid to try something new. It is pride that insists on always being right and always having the answers. You have to be humble enough to ask for and accept help.

Humility demands trust. A lack of trust inevitably means a great deal of fear is present, which comes with a lot of resistance and negative self-talk, such as the following:

- I can't do it.
- I'm not ready.
- It will hurt.
- I'm afraid to talk about my feelings.
- Nobody will like me after really knowing me.
- I don't think I can make it on my own.

- I might fail.
- I'm not good enough.

It is fear that holds us back whenever we struggle with huge obstacles, anything that seems insurmountable, anything that keeps us from peace. Fear is always a function of the lower self, the ego.

At this point, it will be helpful to take time to reflect.

What have you learned about yourself so far? Write down in general terms whatever comes to mind.

_____
_____
_____
_____
_____
_____
_____
_____
_____
_____
_____
_____
_____
_____
_____
_____
_____
_____
_____
_____
_____
_____
_____
_____
_____

Velma Callan Harland

Now, considering all that you have learned and written down, what is most important to you?

3

Releasing Guilt and Shame

This stop on our road trip gives you the opportunity to examine what might be standing in the way of your self-forgiveness. It also gives you a chance to put some additional valuable tools, which you will be able to use for the rest of your life, into your spiritual toolkit.

A common roadblock to self-forgiveness is often guilt. What does your guilt look like? How does it affect you? Guilt can be a healthy, useful, and very functional tool.

However, if months or even years later you are still carrying around the same burden, your guilt has likely become unhealthy and, if that is the case, it is time to do something about it. If you are still judging yourself and telling yourself over and over that you are bad or wrong, you are damaging your self-esteem, which may make it nearly impossible to find compassion for yourself.

Guy Finley, philosopher, author, and former songwriter, has said that judging others is just one of the ways in which our egos maintain the illusion of superiority. Miraculously, when we stop judging others, we no longer judge ourselves, either. If you can learn to stop trying to change others, to accept them totally as they are, you will also learn to accept yourself.

Imagine your thoughts, criticisms, and resentments acting like a boomerang so that all the negative energy you send out comes right back at you. Just for today, make a commitment not to criticize anybody. Enjoy how that feels, and then consider extending that accepting behavior indefinitely.

Ralph Waldo Emerson once said, "The measure of mental health is the disposition to find good everywhere."

Fortunately, we can choose the thoughts we put into our minds. I call this process accessing the higher self or the voice of love.

The point is, if you don't find ways of forgiving yourself, your ego will demand punishment for what you have done and feel guilty about. That will increase your risk of poor mental and/or physical health, including depression.

The tools of the ego are shame, guilt, fear, and blame. When things go wrong, the ego needs to blame someone or something. It uses guilt as the primary weapon to keep us from looking inside. It warns us that if we do look inside, we will find out things about ourselves so dark that no one will be able to love us, and we will certainly not be capable of loving ourselves.

Guilt can also be experienced as chronic anger and resentment toward others. People with a lot of guilt tend to see the world as a hostile and unfair place. They are disconnected from the voice of love or higher self. They are separated from God.

After fifteen years of marriage and three children, Colleen, a medical doctor, became overwhelmed with the responsibilities of caring for her children and carrying the weight of her practice at a new clinic. The eventual result was that she and her husband, Pete, divorced.

Meanwhile, Colleen's sister, Katherine, and Katherine's husband, Adam, had also separated, and they also had three children. It seemed natural at the time for Adam to help Colleen out, driving all the children to sports events and so on. They had always been close as couples, and as time went by, it became easier and easier for Adam and Colleen to be together.

Soon it was evident that things had progressed beyond mere friendship. Even though Colleen fought it and tried to do the right thing (as she put it), it seemed to be beyond her control. She felt she couldn't help herself. The news of their affair devastated the rest of the family.

Colleen and Adam made the decision to marry, move away, and take all six children with them. All the children were of school age.

Things went fairly well for a few years, but then the new marriage also began to crumble. Colleen felt such guilt that she couldn't function properly. Her medical career began to suffer, especially when she began taking prescription drugs and drinking heavily. Adam kept right up with her by using the same crutches.

Colleen was racked with guilt and depressed much of the time. She frequently told herself, "I am worthless and no good."

It would have been much more mature and constructive to say, "I made a grave mistake."

The day finally came when she couldn't take it any more. She sought help for herself and stopped drinking and using drugs. She asked Adam to join her in a treatment program, but he refused; he wasn't ready.

Finally, Colleen began taking responsibility for the pain and suffering she had caused others and herself. With the help of her AA group, she began the process of making amends. She looked deeply at her list of character defects, which always takes great courage. As time went on, she saw the situation with greater and greater clarity. She and Adam separated and eventually divorced.

In time, Colleen came to realize that God had already forgiven her, which made her burden more bearable. Now it was her job to forgive herself. That was the next step, and she longed for the time when she could ask forgiveness from her family.

When, at last, she knew she had done the work and felt strong enough, she asked for that forgiveness and was surprised with the unconditional love she received. Her family saw and understood the enormous effort she was putting into changing her life. They understood the path she was traveling and totally embraced her.

Katherine, her sister and Adam's former wife, had also been in a great deal of pain throughout the whole ordeal. Because her children lived in another city, she was separated from them for long periods of time. She saw them only on some holidays and in the summer. She, too, had decided to try rebuilding her life and was attending university full-time when Colleen, the sister who had married her ex-husband

and taken her children away, came asking for forgiveness. This was Katherine's moment of truth. She was confronted with either forgiving Colleen or staying stuck in her pain and suffering.

She asked herself if she could possibly use the situation as a catalyst to grow and evolve into the person she wanted to be. She chose to forgive Colleen and has since looked upon that time as a period that helped her to grow spiritually.

The two sisters now have a good relationship. They both support their children in every way possible and demonstrate to them by example how to live in a happy and peaceful manner.

Forgiveness is always a process. It is sometimes one step forward and two steps back. It takes commitment and practice—a musician does not get to play at Carnegie Hall without constant practice.

Colleen now does a lot of community work and sponsors others in AA. She says the twelve-step program taught her how to live her life well and to become the kind of person she wanted to be. In other words, she learned to let go and put herself in God's hands.

Colleen's story, of course, is unique to her, just as all our stories are unique, but there is a parallel between her journey and the journey of everyone who lives with profound regret and pain. In Colleen's case, when the pain became too great to bear, she committed herself to looking at her life with clear eyes and an honest heart. She acknowledged her responsibility for what she had done, and that gave her permission to become who she is today. She learned to understand what had motivated her thoughts and behaviors and what had caused her to feel guilty. She sought help and began living in a responsible and loving way. She used her "trust box."

A trust box is a useful tool on the journey to wholeness. It can be any kind of box—wooden or cardboard, homemade or store-bought. One participant in the workshops Colleen attended on self-forgiveness took a cardboard box and covered it with pictures of his favorite golf courses. My own personal trust box is a small wooden box with a key.

The box itself is not that important, but its purpose is, and I encourage you to create a trust box for yourself. Keep it in a place where it will be both accessible and private, because you will be using it frequently for the most personal of items.

Write down on separate pieces of paper all your fears, your guilt, your shame, your anxieties, your need for self-forgiveness, or anything that is bothering you. Place them in your trust box, close the lid, and ask God to help you. Now return to your daily life.

Whenever a particular fear or anxiety returns, go to your box, place your hands on it, and give the problem back to God. This may require going to your trust box hourly in the beginning, but before you realize it, it will have become once a day and, eventually, just once a month or so.

In time, you will be able to remove that particular piece of paper from your box and dispose of it because what you wrote on it will no longer be an issue in your life.

Like Colleen, you have to be able and willing to acknowledge the injuries you have done to yourself. And, also like Colleen, the more you practice being kind and good to yourself, the easier it will become to do the same with others. You have to forgive yourself first. Colleen used her trust box frequently. In fact, she still uses it—but not as often.

When we try to look honestly at ourselves, some of us become confused. We are inclined to think, *I am a mistake*, instead of, *I made a mistake*, or we think, *I am wrong*, instead of, *I did something wrong*. This is called shame. We all experience shame from time to time when we are temporarily embarrassed, but it passes quickly. Toxic shame, on the other hand, stays with us. The antidote for shame is self-praise and self-love.

If a trusted friend sought out your counsel for a situation in which she had responded exactly the same way you had, would you devalue her the same way you have beaten yourself up?

One way to ensure your own guilt is to constantly demand perfection from yourself. Even if you manage to achieve your goals, do you find joy in them? Are they ever quite good enough? If a project is not perfect, at some fundamental level do you feel diminished, a failure? Chronic perfectionism is self-abuse.

If as a child you heard phrases such as the following, you are very likely to experience feelings of inadequacy:

- I don't care what you think or feel.
- Don't bother me.
- What's wrong with you?
- Can't you do anything right?
- You could have gotten an A+ instead of an A.

Pete is a good example of someone striving for perfection. If anyone ever suggested he made a mistake, especially at work, he had to prove that he hadn't, that he was right in whatever he had done. He would e-mail everyone involved to make the point that he had done nothing wrong, sending dates, times, and transcripts of conversations to justify his actions.

For days, he would not be able to think about anything else while he obsessed over the situation. He was always defending himself vigorously and, in fact, he bombarded his co-workers with all his facts and figures, never realizing they found his behavior strange. Even his family suffered.

Although he may not have been able to put his emotions into words, Pete felt he had never had enough love and support from his mother growing up. Fifty years later, he is still trying to prove he is good enough.

Rather than see himself as a worthwhile human being with normal limitations, Pete has held rigid expectations of his own conduct, which has caused him anxiety about the possibility of making mistakes. He has lived by one simple rule: mistakes must be avoided at all costs. When he found himself unable to live up to those unrealistic expectations and felt inadequate and shameful, he beat himself up with his negative self-talk.

Finally, when he just could not continue any longer in this life pattern, he started going to counseling and learned to question his thinking about self-imposed expectations. He learned to identify his rigid beliefs and discover ways to change them.

Today, Pete continues on his journey to recovery. He bought himself some "STOP" stickers and posted them all around the house and on the edges of his computer monitor at work. They serve as reminders to stop the negative self-talk. As well, he uses his trust box regularly and enjoys journaling.

Gradually, Pete is becoming more able to accept his humanness. When he realizes he is reverting to his old thought habits, he changes the channel on his internal TV.

In his forgiveness workshops, Dr. Fred Luskin, author of *Forgive for Good*, says you need to imagine that what you see in your mind is on a TV screen, just like any television program. In your home, you change the channel with your remote control. You choose what programs you want to see. When you want to watch a horror movie, you may have to tune into channel six. To watch a love story, you have to go to channel fourteen. To watch a nature program, you select channel fifty-one. By your control of the remote, you determine what shows up on your TV screen. Now imagine that you have a remote control that changes the channel you are viewing in your mind. For example, a persistent grievance could be seen as having your remote control stuck on the grievance channel. (Luskin 112)

For some of us, the only shows playing on our internal television sets are *I Had Rotten Parents* or *Lousy Rotten Lying Bosses* or *How to Kill My Cheating Spouse and Get Away With It*, or *My Life Is So Unfair*.

The challenge is to reprogram your remote control. Programs on the gratitude channel, beauty channel, love channels and self-forgiveness channels are always available twenty-four hours a day. When our lives are not working as well as we would like them to and we are suffering, that is when we benefit most from tuning into these positive channels.

However, tuning in to the forgiveness, gratitude, beauty, and love channels is more easily said than done. Your remote control may be stuck so that you can't find the beauty or love channels. In that case, you can always watch other people who seem to have really good reception for these channels. Observe how they manage to watch forgiveness channels.

The self-forgiveness and gratitude channels remind us that even though we may be in pain, we do not have to focus all our attention on whatever wound is causing the pain. There is never a moment when you cannot give thanks for the gifts of life. Each breath you take is one such precious gift. Tune into gratitude; it's so much more refreshing and renewing. The world is full of things to appreciate and find beautiful. The only challenge is teaching yourself to see them—to be aware of what's playing in your mind and then switch the channel if necessary.

We are biologically wired to look out for danger, but most of us live in societies and communities in which we are no longer in physical danger all the time. According to Fred Luskin, a study was done at Stanford University in which a number of participants were provided with beepers and were asked to write down whatever they were thinking about when their beepers sounded. Eighty percent of the time, the participants were focused on what was wrong in their lives.

The love and beauty channels remind us that in each and every moment, we have the choice to decide what we will see, hear, and experience, but if you are someone who is in the habit of tuning into the grievance channel, don't despair; any habit can be broken.

Also remember that when you focus only on your problems, your body is under stress, but when you tune into the gratitude, love, beauty, or self-forgiveness channels, you give your body a rest. In fact, when you focus on bringing more positive experiences into your life, your pain diminishes in importance. So, for the next little while, focus only on the good things that happen to you and take special note of the kindness others extend to you and to others.

The one thing no one can take from you is your independence to decide where you will place your attention. You alone control your remote. It is one of the important tools in your taking responsibility for how you feel and one of the beginning steps toward self-forgiveness. Taking responsibility means that even though you may be angry or in pain, you will make the effort to enjoy the good things in life. When you understand that pain is a normal part of life and that all of us have been hurt, you will have a better chance of keeping your suffering in perspective.

On a personal note, when I began taking five to ten minutes twice a day to just sit quietly and concentrate on everything I was grateful for, I experienced a definite shift in my level of happiness. I have gradually increased my meditation time to thirty minutes a day.

To conclude this chapter, write yourself a letter of graduation from guilt and shame. Outline the steps you will take to accept your humanness.

Dear (your name), _____

Velma Callan Harland

End your letter by promising to love and be patient with yourself.

4

Identifying Defense Mechanisms, Anger, and Resentment

We're back on the road again, but we're about to stop at anger and resentment to explore what they mean to our journey to self-forgiveness.

This is the stop where we ask, "What is going on with me?" We do *not* ask what is going on with our boyfriends, girlfriends, spouses, children, mothers, fathers, or anyone else. When we ask, "What is going on with me?" we learn to take responsibility for our own lives. This is where we stop blaming everyone or everything else for whatever we don't like about our lives and present circumstances.

We learned from Colleen that using the trust box is one way of taking responsibility for your actions. When you acknowledge that you need help to change your approach to life and you turn yourself over to God's care, you are then able to learn to be responsible for yourself.

Learning to be responsible for yourself begins with facing your emotions, but first you need to identify them. [2]This may take some time if you have been denying your feelings for a long time, hiding them behind any number of behaviors. Some people use drugs, others use alcohol, inappropriate sexual activities, gambling, overeating, or even compulsive shopping—anything to numb the pain of seeing their circumstances clearly.

Denial is a normal method of self-protection, a psychological defense mechanism. Everyone uses defenses from time to time, and they can

---

[2] See Gayle L. Reed, *Forgiveness; A New Story.*

help for a little while, like shock absorbers, but they are only beneficial in that they provide us with breathing space—time to call upon our inner resources and gain the strength to face the truth.

On the other hand, if denial is used as a coat of armor to protect you indefinitely, your journey to self-forgiveness will probably end up in the ditch. That's why it is vital to identify, face, and deal with the powerful emotions of anger, resentment, and pain.

Other defenses people are tempted to use as coats of armor include suppression, repression, displacement, regression, and diversion.

1. Denial is a defense mechanism in which a person avoids pain by consciously or unconsciously choosing to disbelieve the reality of painful events. Examining and giving up denial can be frightening because that means having to look more closely at the anger and pain underneath, which you don't want to do. Denial can be useful in an emergency, but if it is used for any length of time, it can prevent you from moving forward.
2. Suppression is an early form of denial in which a person consciously and actively attempts to push painful thoughts and feelings out of his mind. This is done by throwing oneself into an overload of projects or, as mentioned before, by using drugs and/or alcohol, excessive exercise, and so on—activities that keep thoughts and feelings below the surface. Unfortunately, suppressed feelings are likely to surface in unpleasant ways, such as in relationship difficulties, anxiety, and/or depression.
3. Repression is a common defense mechanism that happens automatically and unconsciously. It is not like suppression or denial in which a person is initially aware of painful feelings. It is, instead, a way of immediately and automatically removing from consciousness any thoughts or feelings that are unacceptable or frightening. When a person is living with repression and is asked about her well being, her response is almost always, "I'm fine," even though she may actually be living in chaos.

Repression that blocks uncomfortable feelings of anger and underlying pain does not go away as time goes by, which can be very damaging. Repressed anger can cause a person to become numb.

4. Displacement is the defense mechanism of placing blame where it does not belong. When a person unconsciously blames someone else for his own feelings of anger and pain, that could be displacement. It is denying personal responsibility for certain behaviors by insisting the responsibility lies with someone or something else.
5. Regression occurs when a person returns to patterns of thinking, feeling, or behaving that belong to an earlier, less threatening period of life. It is an attempt to return to a time when life was easier. If left unexamined, regression can continue to distort decision-making into the future.
6. Diversion, which is self-evident and quite common, is changing the subject to avoid a topic that is threatening.

Now, consider each of the following questions and answer them as fully and truthfully as possible.

1. Do you use defense mechanisms to avoid looking at your anger and underlying pain? If so, what behaviors do you use? In what situations do you use them? Explain.

_____
_____
_____
_____
_____
_____
_____
_____

Velma Callan Harland

You may have heard the story of the man who was furiously rowing his boat to shore to beat the storm that was coming. He wasn't getting anywhere because there was an old rusty anchor holding the boat from moving, but he didn't realize it. Repressed anger is like that; it stands in the way of self-forgiveness like a rusty anchor.

2. What is stopping you from getting to shore? What does your old rusty anchor look like?

_____
_____
_____
_____
_____
_____
_____
_____
_____
_____
_____
_____
_____
_____

3. When you use a defense mechanism, is it helping you, or do you still feel anxious, sad, or exhausted?

_____
_____
_____
_____
_____
_____
_____
_____
_____
_____
_____
_____
_____
_____

Anger, when expressed in constructive ways, is a natural and necessary emotion to ensure that justice, and perhaps some other principles, are not trampled. Anger can motivate us to make positive changes in our situations.

However, when anger is not expressed constructively, it can be like a raging fire, causing you to explode and feel totally out of control. Sometimes a display of anger is an announcement that you are out of control and that you don't have good skills with which to handle the situation. Then, rather than protecting you from your past, it becomes your jailer.

Resentment, on the other hand, turns anger into something stiff, tough, and rigid. Resentment is like cement hardening all around you, like that suit of armor. It keeps you stuck, unable to move forward and enjoy life.

By replacing your unresolved anger with resentment again and again, you become bitter and isolated. Resentments can make you feel as if you are always on edge, which sometimes results in taking frustrations out on the wrong people.

Anger has been described as a raging fire, while resentment is the smoldering coals, ready to erupt as soon as someone stirs them.

Jerry, a young man I recently worked with, phoned to tell me about an episode of anger he had just experienced. He said he had been playing a game on his computer. When he lost the game, he became so angry he picked up a chair, intending to throw it at the computer. He was startled at how the anger had just appeared out of the blue.

Then he told me what he did. As he was standing there with the chair in his hands, he heard himself say, "Stop!" Asking himself what the anger was all about, he immediately took a few deep breaths, put the chair down, found a paper and pen, and started writing.

By the way, taking several deep breaths is particularly effective when dealing with out-of-control anger. It does, however, take determination and practice.

Jerry came to understand through his writing that he was still blaming himself for the mistakes he had made when he had used drugs. Together, we went over a few strategies for him to use in order to process the pain, including taking the time to really feel his anger and ask himself, "What does my pain look like?"

His next step was to relax and listen to what the pain told him.

Another tool for processing pain is a visualization technique that can also be used for stress management. Imagine standing at the edge of the ocean. You see a series of waves coming toward you and feel they may overwhelm you with their intensity and power. However, they won't if you ask God to stand there with you as you let each wave come . . . and then let it go.

As we watch each wave crest and diminish, we know that our pain, too, will pass. Just notice and accept the feeling. Watch as it gradually diminishes. In this process, you can develop an inner core of peace that keeps you from being destroyed by fear and confusion.

The attitudes, feelings, and behaviors you have today are often largely the direct result of experiences and messages you had in your early environment. Perhaps you grew up in chaos or never learned appropriate decision-making skills or understood that every behavior brings a consequence.

It is important to understand that you are not to blame because you struggle with anger. You are not a bad person because you experience anger, though you may be a person in pain. Anger is a way of coping. It helps for a little while in overcoming hurt and helplessness. Anger is a response we learn early in life to help us cope with pain, but it can also become a habit beyond its usefulness. Fortunately, habits can be broken.

Angry people often hate themselves. If you feel you would like to acquire new anger-management skills, I suggest you obtain Matthew McKay and Peter Rogers's *The Anger Control Workbook*, which contains many well thought-out strategies and techniques.

List the three most negative thoughts you most often have about yourself.

_____
_____
_____
_____
_____
_____
_____
_____
_____
_____
_____
_____
_____

Who are you angry with? Why?

_____
_____
_____
_____
_____
_____
_____
_____
_____
_____
_____
_____
_____

Who or what do you resent?

_____
_____
_____
_____
_____
_____
_____
_____
_____
_____
_____
_____
_____

Now, list at least three positive things about yourself. (Please don't skip this exercise. It is too important. If you can't get started, ask someone you trust for help.)

_____
_____
_____
_____
_____
_____
_____
_____
_____
_____
_____
_____
_____

Sara is a fifty-year-old woman who was married to a prominent civil servant. They had a comfortable, upper-middle-class income. Sara had always been a stay-at-home mom with their two children. She was not particularly happy in the marriage, however, though she enjoyed her social status.

When Steve told Sara he was leaving her for his younger girlfriend, Sara was devastated. She had no idea that Steve had been carrying on an affair.

Her response was, "How can you do this to me? My life is over. I am so embarrassed. You have to come back and make it up to the children and me."

When it became clear that the situation was not going to change, Sara began seeking revenge. She refused to let the children, twelve and sixteen, have anything to do with their father and managed to persuade them that their father didn't love them. If he did, she said, he would never have left them.

The financial settlement turned into a horror story because Sara refused to agree to any reasonable offers that Steve and his lawyers presented. She was out for revenge, and she was determined to get it. She felt she was right and was going to prove it, and in the process she was going to take Steve for everything he had.

Now, seven years later, nothing has changed in Sara's thinking or behavior. She still has the same conversation with whoever still listens to her. However, fewer and fewer friends will have much to do with her. The children are still alienated from their father in spite of Steve's best efforts to be in contact with them.

When her marriage failed, Sara was filled with fear that life wouldn't bring her what she thought she needed or wanted. Many of her actions and choices came about because she was afraid of losing what she already had, even though she wasn't particularly happy with her life.

If she had explored her responsibility in the breakdown of the marriage, events might have unfolded differently. Had she noticed they were growing apart emotionally and physically, perhaps she might have considered forgiving herself for her contribution to the eventual divorce, and then she could have gone on to forgive Steve for his behavior. When forgiveness was suggested to Sara, she immediately resisted.

"Why should I be the one to forgive when I am right and he has hurt us all so badly?" she asked.

But Sara was mistaken. Forgiveness is a gift of kindness to ourselves, not to the other person. She missed the point that after all those years, she was the one carrying the burden of anger and pain wherever she went.

She didn't understand that the hurt feelings, the angry thoughts, and the knot in the pit of her stomach whenever she thought about the divorce were causing her to feel badly, not what happened in the past. It is her reaction to it today that causes this continuing problem.

Resentment is a bad habit that can cause you to distrust your judgment and to think and act in ways that go against your value system or moral code. Noticing how you begin to develop resentment is a very important part of learning to live with less anger.

We often become resentful about the things that people do or don't do that are contrary to our expectations. Think about your resentments.

Have your resentments caused you to take actions you are not proud of? Write about this for a few minutes.

_____
_____
_____
_____
_____
_____
_____
_____
_____

List the names of the people you're feeling resentful toward, and write about what happened or did not happen that you now resent.

As we continue our road trip, we will explore ways to change how you think by challenging old ideas that might be keeping you hostile and trapped in resentment.

5
Seeing Things Differently

This is where we stop the car, take our shovel out of the trunk, and begin digging in earnest to clearly uncover our behaviors and liabilities. Don't be discouraged as you dig because, along with some lumps of coal, you are going to uncover some unexpected diamonds.

You may already recognize some of your personal patterns and more clearly see some of the negative consequences of the choices you have made. Keep working on becoming completely honest with yourself as you face your attitudes to life's challenges.

Some of us find it hard to identify our emotions, but it is important to do so and to understand them. One of the best ways to move toward self-forgiveness is to accept and learn to handle your emotions. Anger, fear, resentment, anxiety, despair, and sadness can provide us with important information about ourselves.

Visualize a pipeline running through your body from the top of your head down and out through your toes. Your normal human emotions run through this pipeline. The system usually works well, but sometimes the pipeline becomes clogged . . . and you know what a mess it can be when a toilet or the kitchen sink backs up!

Now imagine that your negative emotions are causing the blockage. What can you do to unclog your emotional pipeline?

First, ask yourself what you are feeling. Are you angry, hurt, glad, sad, ashamed, or something else? Then go deeper into the experience. Meet it head on and see what it is all about rather than try to eliminate it from your life because it causes anxiety. Trying to avoid anything that might distress you is not a good strategy. When you keep trying to avoid difficulties, eventually you will constantly look over your shoulder, waiting for the other shoe to drop, worried that something will catch up with you.

Next, be careful not to blame anyone else for your feelings. The emotions are yours, and so is the response to them that *you* choose. If you identify that you are angry and then blame your mother, your spouse, difficulties in your workplace, or anything outside of yourself, you are being counterproductive.

We all have feelings. Feelings are a part of us. We don't have to deny or judge them. Just accept them as okay.

Sharing your feelings with someone you trust can keep pressure from building up and help you let go. Express yourself in a healthy manner, but also be careful not to talk about it over and over.

Two women, Margaret and Sophie, had horrific car accidents on the same day. They both had to be removed from their vehicles with the Jaws of Life. They both needed hospitalization in the following weeks. Even nine months later, they were both still encountering health problems and facing surgery.

Both women had their expenses and salaries paid by an insurance company and hoped for a large settlement, which they felt they needed and deserved.

Sophie understood that such a financial settlement could end up in the courts and take a long time to settle, so she made a conscious choice to let all the frustration and negativity go. She decided she would rather put her energy into getting well and healing her body. Shortly after she made that choice, she received a large cash settlement, and her health was eventually completely restored.

Margaret, on the other hand, chose to fight the insurance company for as large a settlement as possible. From the very beginning, the company had been paying her expenses and her full salary as an executive secretary, but when faced with her suit for a larger settlement, the company launched a counter-suit demanding return of all the payments made to her to date! It became their view that Margaret had been able to resume work, which she claimed to be unable to do. The company put her under surveillance for weeks and videotaped her going shopping and carrying on with her daily activities. The matter is still before the courts.

It is never the event itself, but the reaction to the event that makes the difference. Whenever we put our attention on our pain and anger instead of on the need to move beyond them, that is exactly what we get back—more pain and anger. This is an illustration of the saying, "What goes around comes around."

Both Sophie and Margaret suffered car accidents. They both thought about what had happened to them but then evaluated the circumstances differently. In response to their thoughts, they had different emotional reactions.

It isn't events or other people or things that cause our emotions. It is the thoughts we have about an event or situation that cause our feelings.

Personal Beliefs

All of us have a set of general rules we live by, but *some people cause themselves unnecessary pain and frustration by holding unrealistic or irrational beliefs.* Which of the following best fits your personal beliefs?

- Things outside my control cause my unhappiness.
- There is little I can do to feel better.
- Many external factors are outside my control, but it is my thoughts, not those external factors, that cause my feelings, and I can learn to control my thoughts.
- Events in my past are the cause of my problems, and they continue to influence me now.
- To be worthwhile, I must succeed at everything I do.

- I need love and approval from those significant to me; I must avoid disapproval from any source.
- I must worry about things that could be dangerous, unpleasant, or frightening; otherwise they might happen.

Forgiving ourselves is probably one of the greatest challenges we ever face. It is the process of learning to love and accept ourselves no matter what. Love and self-forgiveness are the same thing.

The more harshly you judge others, the more critical you will be of yourself. People are most likely to be critical of others in areas in which they are weakest, which is often too painful for them to acknowledge. However, if you can do so, you will begin to change and correct the parts of yourself that aren't working. If you don't, if you refuse to learn the lessons your relationships are trying to teach you, you will attract the same types of people into your life over and over again.

A good example of this occurred at a meeting I attended not long ago. Orville announced to the group that he "just couldn't stand Jim," because Jim was so loud and overbearing. The others around the table couldn't resist exchanging knowing looks and laughing out loud. Orville was confused by this, not realizing that what he criticized in another person was also his own most glaring fault.

Is there someone in your life who causes you to cringe every time you see her; someone who you just can't stand to be around? Write down that person's name and list everything you find unacceptable about him or her. What is it about this person that you find most upsetting, most disturbing? For example, is he judgmental, conceited, arrogant, self-centered, greedy? Does she have a need for power and control? Is he jealous and competitive? Be totally honest. Feel the emotions as you write.

_____
_____
_____

Now go back over your list with the knowledge that anything you resent and strongly react to in another person is also in you. Make a new list of what you can learn about yourself from your dislike of this person.

_____
_____
_____
_____
_____
_____
_____

Last thing at night before going to sleep, I like to do a mini-review of the day's events. I silently observe, without judgment, all that took place during the day. I witness my vulnerabilities, judgments, anxieties, and the opinions I have expressed. In this way, I process my own behaviors and see the consequences of my actions.

This tool of detached observation, or witnessing, helps me become more deeply aware of who I am and how I am. Through it, I learn to respond differently, if necessary. I must warn you, however; it is not an easy process.

Once you have completed this step of honestly recognizing things about yourself that you found difficult to acknowledge before, you will have reached a new plateau on the journey and can start to use every relationship in your life to reflect on what is going on inside you.

Up to now, you have been examining your past so that you can effectively change your attitudes and behaviors in the present and future. You have seen how they can cause you harm as well as harm others.

How have you caused yourself harm in the past?

_____
_____
_____

How have you caused others harm in the past?

_____
_____
_____
_____
_____
_____

In chapter 2 we talked about humility. We found that being willing to forgive ourselves, as well as others, requires a generous dose of humility. This doesn't mean you must agree with everyone about everything. It simply means you can choose to stop resenting others and wishing harm to those you perceive as having harmed you.

Apologizing is often appropriate, but apologies do not always mend a situation. When we apologize, we sometimes find ourselves using over-the-top explanations for our behavior. On the other hand, making amends suggests that we are ready and willing to take action to change that behavior.

George, a manager with a large department store chain, had been asked to take charge of an important seminar involving all the department managers. George meticulously prepared for the seminar, devising questions to ensure the active participation of his colleagues.

When the seminar was well underway, he noticed that few were paying attention and that many were not responding to his questions. He lost his cool. He berated his colleagues and humiliated several other managers, as well as himself, in the process. He felt out of control and burnt out as he left the seminar, knowing his behavior had been completely inappropriate.

George replayed this experience over and over in his mind for two days and came to the realization that he must somehow make amends for what he had done. He thoughtfully made a list of the people he had damaged—not an easy task. He felt resistance as he realized he had to make face-to-face admissions of guilt to those he had humiliated, but he had no idea how his actions would be received by his colleagues.

Even though George's personal life was in shambles (he was in the middle of a nasty divorce and had creditors pursuing him), he wanted to take responsibility for his actions without offering excuses. As a final preparation, he prayed about what he planned to say.

Finally, George set up a meeting with Bill, the first person he wanted to make amends with. He expressed his genuine regret for his unacceptable behavior. Bill's response surprised and relieved him.

"I was a little concerned about you," Bill replied. "I hope you're okay."

Conversations with the others also went well. George told me he had vacillated between minimizing his behavior and trying to get out of taking responsibility for his actions. Deep down, he knew he had to do the honorable thing and be honest with others and himself.

"As soon as I came clean," he told me, "I could feel the humiliation and shame lift."

George knew that even though it had been a difficult process to prepare for, it was a necessary step for him to take in order to achieve the peace and serenity he was seeking.

George then took some time off work to reevaluate his life. He did not want a repeat of his previous behavior. He began seeing a spiritual counselor and took steps to relieve the stress in his life.

If you are considering making amends with someone, several things must be taken into account, and discussing the situation with a trusted advisor is often helpful.

If someone continues to suffer because of your actions, or you are still hurting, it may be wise to postpone making amends for awhile to be certain you don't cause more harm. Timing is everything.

If someone has died or is in poor health, you can still make amends. You can write a letter but not mail it. And, by the way, please don't forget to write a letter of amends to yourself.

Books, articles, and Internet searches can all provide many good resources for anyone wanting more guidelines for making amends, but you have to be ready. It is impossible to drive north and south at the same time. However, a negative thought or feeling can be canceled by thinking a positive one.

Dr. Fred Luskin, co-founder and director of the Stanford University Forgiveness Project, teaches a technique he calls PERT in his workshops and writes about it in his book *Forgive for Good*. (120)

- Bring your attention fully to your stomach as you slowly draw in two deep breaths. As you inhale, allow the air to gently push your belly out. As you exhale, consciously relax your belly so that it feels soft.
- On the third full and deep inhalation, bring to your mind's eye an image of someone you love or of a beautiful scene in nature that fills you with awe and wonder.(120) (Often people have a stronger response when they imagine their positive feelings are centred in the area around their heart.)
- While practicing, continue with soft belly breathing. Ask the relaxed and peaceful part of you what you can do to resolve your difficulty.

Dr. Luskin says this technique can help us if we practice it the moment a painful experience comes to mind. We need to learn how to maintain our peace in any situation, no matter how upsetting. Use this technique whenever and wherever you feel anger, hurt, depression, or bitterness.

"PERT is the most powerful technique I know to help you remain in control of your emotions," says Dr. Luskin. (120)

Another technique also involves breathing. When you find you are beginning to feel upset with yourself, use that as a cue to employ this technique right away. Remember, you are changing your behavior, which is not easy to do.

Take a deep breath through your nose slowly to the count of four; hold to the count of four, and breathe out through your mouth, again, to the count of four. Do this six or seven times to ground yourself, and then breathe slowly, still inhaling through your nose and exhaling through your mouth. As you inhale, breathe in calmness and gratitude for all the good things in your life, and as you exhale, let go of all your negative feelings and emotions.

The more you use this technique, the better it works. Of course, it won't work if you don't remember to use it. People sometimes wear a rubber band on their wrists, and when they realize they are indulging in negative thinking, they snap the band as a reminder to change their habit by using one of their new techniques.

Cynthia Jordan writes in the newsletter *Intuitive Flash* that scientists now have conducted studies to show us how powerful our thoughts are and how they affect our minds and bodies. For example, Dr. Masaru Emoto, author of several books and director of the IHM General Research Institute, has done extensive research on water. In fact, he has discovered that thoughts and feelings are powerful enough to affect the properties of water.

Dr. Emoto began photographing the ice crystals that formed in different types of water and found that the shape of the crystals changed depending on what the water had been exposed to. He has published many of these photographs in his book, *The Hidden Messages in Water*. These photographs reveal that pure spring water formed into beautiful symmetrical crystals while the crystals in polluted water were incomplete and deformed—or crystals failed to form at all!

Dr. Emoto expanded his research to include water exposed to different types of music and found that heavy metal music, for instance, caused the water to form shapes similar to that of polluted water, while classical music caused the formation of beautiful symmetrical shapes similar to that of pure water.

He further expanded his research to include water exposed to thoughts and emotions written on pieces of paper and taped to the water container. To his amazement, the water responded to the words "love" and "gratitude," or other positive sentiments, by forming beautiful crystals in symmetrical shapes. Water shown the words "you fool," or other negative thoughts, responded with malformed and fragmented shapes.

Jordan continues writing, it was "awe inspiring" to see the photographs of these crystals and realize that water can respond to thoughts and emotions. "At the same time," she wrote, "it is almost frightening to realize how much power is held in our thoughts and emotions."

Here is one more example of the effect our thoughts and emotions have on our quality of life. Peggy McColl, author of *Your Destiny Switch*, tells about a seminar she attended where motivational speaker Bob Proctor placed two clear glasses on a table, each half full. One had coffee in it, and the other contained water. Bob took a teaspoon of water and stirred it into the glass that held the coffee, but Peggy could not see any change in it. He mixed in another teaspoonful of water, and another and another. It wasn't until he had added several spoonfuls that Peggy began to observe the coffee becoming slightly more transparent.

Bob explained that this represented the effect of positive emotions on a person who has a negative state of mind. It takes a while for results to show.

Then Bob stirred one teaspoonful of the coffee into the glass of clear water. Instantly, Peggy perceived the liquid changing color. Bob explained that this was the effect of negativity on a positive mind. It's like a tiny bit of poison and has an almost immediate effect.

Feelings don't just go away. They can stay around and take other forms. For example, feelings can become an attitude. Instead of just feeling angry, you can become an angry person.

What feelings have led to your mistakes, regardless of whether you later made amends for them?

_____

What new behaviors do you need to develop in order to increase your ability to forgive yourself?

_____

Old habits die hard. Concentrating on the positive characteristics you want to develop gives you momentum and points you in the right direction . . . one spoonful at a time!

6

Prayer and Meditation

Throughout this book, we have been exploring our willingness to change our behaviors and attitudes. We have also been doing the work that will make us more receptive to the idea of God, or a higher power, doing for us what we cannot do for ourselves.

Throughout this process, little by little, we begin to grow spiritually. Our spiritual foundation helps us to make decisions about our conduct and guides us along our daily journeys. Self-forgiveness—in fact, any attitude of forgiveness—is a spiritual phenomenon.

One of the most effective ways of encouraging the development of spirituality is to take time for prayer and meditation every day. When you commit to this practice, whether or not you actually feel like it in the moment, you will acquire a habit that will broaden the channel for positive change in your life—for God's action.

In the beginning, you might simply pray for willingness to develop this habit of daily prayer and meditation. Ask to be given more faith if it is lacking. Ask to be more forgiving of others and yourself.

Attitude always precedes behavior. Therefore, if you can remain faithful to practicing a daily routine of prayer, you will find, before you know it, that prayer has become a habit.

If you are concerned because you don't know how to pray, don't worry. I know of many people who feel they don't pray properly, but prayer is very personal. I don't believe anyone can do it wrong. It can be as simple as a conversation with God.

I would never presume to tell anyone how to pray. I will only give you my experience and relate to you what others do and have said about prayer.

One of my favorite times to pray is while I am taking a long walk alone, mostly in the mornings. This is one of the times when I feel I am really connected to an "inner guidance." When I get home, I open my journal and start to write. This is my morning prayer, my way of having a conversation with God. I don't worry about punctuation, spelling, or editing. I just bring everything to God. No matter how I am feeling, I just put it all down on paper. It's a lovely way to start my day, and I always end my morning writing by thanking God for the blessings in my life.

My friend Adam tells me that when he is jogging, he finds it easier to pray because he becomes lost in the rhythm of his pace.

Marcel, who is a devout Catholic, uses a form of prayer that is more structured. He gets up every morning, sits in his favorite rocking chair, and reads from Scripture or his favorite prayer book. He reads very slowly, usually aloud, and thinks about every word he is reading. He takes his time and lets it really sink in.

After he has finished reading, Marcel tries to sit quietly and just listen. He then asks himself if any of the reading spoke to him. Then he usually goes back and rereads the same piece.

"Sometimes," he tells me, "I can't find any meaning, so I just go on to reading the next part."

During the day, he thinks about the topic and mulls it over some more.

My dear friend, Lois, has a different approach. She writes:

> For me, prayer is a matter of awareness. By that, I mean an ongoing consciousness of God's presence, no matter what I am doing. Quite apart from my daily prayer periods, morning greeting, mealtime thanksgiving, and evening review of what has unfolded this day, I make an effort to remember that God is present in the people I meet (even the annoying ones), in the tasks I perform (even the tiresome ones), and in the glories of nature. It helps to know I can complain to Him at any time

or give thanks for small, unexpected blessings, as I would with any other loved one.

Awareness is a state of mind I have cultivated over a number of years and, though I acknowledge that it gets easier as I mature, I don't think it's ever too early to start practising.

Another technique I personally find helpful is the use of a mantra. Throughout history, many religious traditions have used some sort of mantra as a gateway to centering prayer or meditation. A mantra is a prayer word or phrase from Scripture or some other source that has meaning for you. It is repeated, slowly and prayerfully, in harmony with your breathing, over and over, creating an atmosphere of calm so you can focus and center yourself.

I create my own mantras; each one is a breath prayer of seven syllables. For example, "I know I am forgiven." I breathe in on the first three syllables and breathe out on the last three. The middle syllable is the change between breathing in and breathing out.

When using a mantra, some people have found it easier to focus on an empty space, a candle flame, a rock, a flower, or some simple object. I usually just close my eyes. I stay in prayer this way for ten to fifteen minutes.

Often people will say, "I just can't meditate." Usually, these are the people who would benefit most from the practice. It is just like exercising any muscle in your body. The more you use it, the stronger and better it becomes. What people don't realize is that when they place their attention on their worries or things that haven't worked out, they are meditating. What we think, we become. When we meditate on what is positive, we are working on changing our thought patterns in positive ways.

Ralph, a student friend of mine, says he meditates every day at the same time and in the same place, as consistently as he possibly can. He says this practice enhances a sense of sacredness for him.

He always begins by sitting comfortably in a chair with his back straight. Then he closes his eyes and focuses on his breathing, following his breath as it goes through his nostrils into his chest and down into his lungs. He focuses on one breath at a time, and if he finds his mind wandering, he does not get upset about it; he just watches his thoughts pass by as if they were on a movie screen.

Then Ralph visualizes bringing the rays of the sun into every cell of his body as he inhales. As he exhales, he visualizes a gray mist leaving his body through his mouth. This mist carries all his negative thoughts and feelings with it. Ralph keeps on breathing this way until his body feels as limp as a wet rag and he is totally relaxed. He continues for fifteen to twenty minutes.

Ralph says meditating in this way teaches him gentleness and a way of forgiving himself for his mistakes and brings peace to his life.

Others who would like to experience this form of meditation may find it easier to sit on the floor with cushions propping them up instead of sitting upright in a chair. Some even find it more comfortable to lie down. Just try not to fall asleep.

I want to give you an example of a guided imagery prayer. Imagine yourself in a place that is ugly and confining. Acknowledge that you do not like to be there. Notice everything around you. Touch the walls and any objects you see. What do you hear? Do you smell any odors?

What part of you does this room represent? Are the walls made of fear, confining you? Are they a compulsion that binds you? Is this a place where you can't forgive yourself or others, a place of betrayals, a vault of pride, a den of self-hatred?

Name what it is that confines you and surrounds you. Can you forgive yourself for whatever holds you in this place? Can you accept yourself?

Take time to consider this, and if you are not able to forgive and accept yourself, pray to be able to do so. Can you reach out to touch this place again with forgiveness, even love?

Now imagine the place is filling with a soft and glowing light. This light is surrounding you and penetrating you. Feel it reach every part of your body. From within the light, hear your God say, "I am with you. I love you. I forgive you. I will be your strength."

What a relief. We share with God our deepest, darkest secrets and find we no longer have to live with an ever-present threat of exposure. It takes humility to say to your creator,

- I now can see how petty jealousies and resentments have colored my relationship with my brother.
- Why couldn't I have been a better and kinder daughter?
- How can I ever forgive myself for what I have done?

It takes humility, yes, and yet it is that acknowledgment that puts you in a right relationship with your God. Now, with God's help, you are ready and willing to change your behavior.

I met Kate and Don at a self-forgiveness workshop in California. This young couple had recently lost a child to illness, and they were struggling with the most difficult task of trying to forgive themselves after experiencing such a devastating loss. They were in the initial stages of blaming themselves for not being able to save their little girl, Amy. They were asking questions, such as,

- Why didn't we ask for a second opinion?
- What did we do wrong?
- Why didn't we take her to the hospital sooner?

They were beating themselves up over and over again. They said they hated themselves and felt paralyzed with anxiety. We became fast friends and have kept in touch since our time in California. I recently received a letter from them, and I asked their permission to share their journey.

In their search for answers to their questions, Kate and Don began investigating the world's spiritual traditions. They found that in the previous few years there had been an increased interest in and acceptance of reincarnation. The idea that the soul is eternal and lives on forever is a part of most spiritual traditions, but the idea that people, when they die, reincarnate into other personalities is an essential part of reincarnation. The basic spiritual concept is that we all live through different lifetimes. Our lives on earth are seen as different classrooms where we learn the lessons we need to, the lessons that will move us forward spiritually.

Don went to a past-life regression therapist who hypnotized him. He was told that he had had a long life with Amy in several past lives, but this time around, Amy had chosen an early death because she had completed her lessons—accomplished her mission for this lifetime.

This knowledge changed both Kate's and Don's beliefs. They became much more peaceful about this lifetime's problems and difficulties. Kate said this knowledge helped her see that she was no longer the helpless victim who never had to assume responsibility for her own happiness. They were finally able to arrive at acceptance, and they found that the experience had a positive, healing effect.

To end this chapter, spend some time thinking about your own spiritual journey and your concept of God, your higher power.

How do you understand God?

_____
_____
_____
_____
_____
_____
_____
_____
_____

What methods can you use to be more in touch with yourself, your values, and your higher power?

7

Getting There—Formulating a Plan and Putting It All Together

Because self-love and self-forgiveness are the same thing, you need to shower yourself with tender loving care. This may be a foreign concept to you, but think of it this way: A young mother breastfeeding her newborn infant is told by her doctor that she is starving the child because she isn't getting proper nourishment herself. He insists that the young mother look after herself first, because if she doesn't, she will never be capable of looking after anyone else. Now, doesn't that make sense?

I can't tell you how many people I have come across who live exactly the way this young mother was living—always putting others first and neglecting themselves. Don't make the same mistake.

Often, participants in my workshops bring me articles and exercises that we use in class. I don't know the original source of this one, but it is called *Becoming Your Own Friend.*

Imagine what it would be like to live with someone who constantly judges you as wrong, bad, weak, or stupid for the things you have done. This would, in all likelihood, undermine your confidence and/or motivation to make the changes you want to make in your life.

Now, imagine instead that you make choices that are not what you really want for yourself, but you live with a kind, wise, and insightful person who can clearly see when you make poor choices. Instead of emotionally and mentally beating you down for them, she offers you love and acceptance. At the same time, this person helps you look at your choices with a new clarity, compassion, and wisdom.

Imagine that this kind person supports you in seeing the fears and conditioning that motivate you. She understands that your choices, even self-destructive ones, are attempts to find relief, peace, and happiness. She knows and wants you to know that coming from the degree of inner fear and separation that you come from, you do the best you can. But your kind friend assures you that there are other choices you can make, and the way to start is by being gentle with yourself. She encourages you to accept support from a higher power and from others. She tells you that there truly is grace in your life but that only you can let it in.

Imagine what it would be like if you befriended yourself in the same way as this kind of person. Repeat this suggestion many times in the days ahead—become a true friend to yourself.

While working through this book, you have been exposed to a number of skills and practices. Reviewing them at this point will help to clarify and solidify them for you.

Have you begun journaling yet? How is it helping you?

_____
_____
_____
_____
_____
_____
_____
_____
_____
_____

Do you have your trust box? How have you used it?

Have you begun to identify all that you are grateful for in your life? Keep track of all your blessings by recording them daily. List some new things you are grateful for, including experiences and people, below.

_____
_____
_____
_____
_____
_____
_____
_____
_____
_____
_____
_____
_____
_____
_____

Have you been using your remote control to change the channel on your internal television set? Replaying over and over again in your head what you want to forgive yourself for only makes you feel worse. Instead, whenever you find yourself doing that, hit the stop button and refocus on something positive.

Have you been able to identify your emotions and feelings more clearly than before?

Have you posted your STOP stickers around your home and workplace? Remember to use this technique, as well as the rubber band on your wrist, as cues to change your focus when you need to.

Have you remembered in difficult situations to say, "Stop!" and do some breathing exercises?

Have you been able to incorporate the wave exercise when needed?

Have you been able to focus on and identify some of your good characteristics? Explain.

_____
_____
_____
_____
_____
_____
_____
_____
_____
_____
_____
_____
_____
_____
_____

Have you been able to substitute positive thinking for your negative thoughts? What specifically did you do?

_____
_____
_____
_____
_____
_____
_____
_____
_____
_____
_____
_____
_____
_____
_____

Have you discovered new insights about yourself? Explain.

_____
_____
_____
_____
_____
_____
_____
_____
_____
_____
_____
_____

Have you gone over the "relationships as mirrors" exercise again? Have you made amends to others and to yourself? Have you been using any form of prayer and meditation? Have you tried using affirmations?

Do you know that by the time we are adults we have hours and hours of negative tapes playing in our heads? Doing affirmations allows us to begin replacing our negative self-talk with more positive ideas and concepts. For example, I often use, "I forgive myself."

Doing affirmations just ten minutes a day can counterbalance years of old bad habits. Try to be really conscious of what you are telling yourself. Suspend any doubts you may have about how effective this practice is and put your full mental and emotional energy into it. Word your affirmations in the present tense and always in the most positive way you can. Here are a couple of suggestions:

- I am capable of changing.
- Just for today, I am acting in ways that I admire in (person's name).
- The Christ within me is creating miracles in my life now.

Studies show that people who are unforgiving have more health problems and a quality of hardness that seems to say, "I'm not going to let that go."

Another really good way to take care of yourself is to seek out those things that make you laugh and promote positive feelings. Every time you laugh is like a miracle pill for your health. According to doctors,[3] laughter can reduce stress, lower blood pressure, boost the immune system, and protect the heart.

My good friend Susan did exactly that. She was going through a particularly difficult divorce. Everything that could go wrong went wrong, and then some. She used to say she had five dependants: her two children, her lawyer, her husband, and her husband's lawyer.

The day she got an extremely large bill from her lawyer, she sat down at her computer to type an invoice for him. Under fees she listed the following:

- Stress and anguish regarding post-traumatic stress disorder.
- Preparation of this invoice.
- Disbursements: postage and envelope.
- Total amount due: $30.5 million.

I don't know about her lawyer, but several of Susan's friends had a good dose of laughter over her invoice.

---

[3] Tugade, M. *The Undoing Affect of Positive Emotions*

8

Learn to Relax

Learning to relax is critical to your success on the journey to self-forgiveness and peace. The following technique has been around a very long time. In fact, it has been used for years in yoga classes. It may seem really simple and easy to you, so much so that you might dismiss even trying it, but let me assure you, it is worth the time and effort. The goal is to enable you to scan your body for tension and then be able to release that tension anytime, anywhere, in about thirty seconds.

This particular version is based loosely on the explanation in the *Anger Control Workbook* by Matthew McKay and Peter Rodgers.

The basic principle is to first increase the tension in your muscles, hold it for five to seven seconds, and then relax. Remember to focus on one set of muscles at a time. Repeat each procedure as many times as necessary to achieve the desired effect. (Caveat: Do not tense areas of physical pain, injury, or recent surgery. Remove contact lenses.)

Get into a comfortable position, lying down or in a chair. Allow yourself to experience a comfortable feeling of heaviness. Start at the bottom and, stretching your legs, point your toes away from your body, noting the tension in your ankles.

Now point your toes toward your head, creating tension in your calves. Let your feet fall to the floor. Take a deep breath, and relax.

Now tighten your buttocks, and then your thighs by pressing down on your heels as hard as you can. Hold the tension for five to seven seconds. Then let go, take a deep breath, and relax.

Next, take a deep breath, filling your lungs completely, and flex your chest muscles. Now tighten your stomach muscles, creating, in effect, a coat of armor. Hold, exhale, and relax.

Now arch your back, as though it were a bow. Avoid straining, and keep the rest of your body as relaxed as possible. Notice the tension beginning down your tailbone and moving all the way up your spine to your neck. Hold as long as possible, then slump forward, take a deep breath, and relax.

Bend your elbows and tense your forearms and biceps in the classic Charles Atlas pose. Clench your fists at the same time. Tense these muscles until they feel taut. Then straighten out your arms, shake out your hands, take a deep breath, and relax.

Now hunch your shoulders and pull your head in like a turtle. Press your chin against your chest, tightening your throat. Experience this uncomfortable sensation, then drop your shoulders and allow your head to fall forward. Now, slowly and carefully, roll your head to the side as far as you can comfortably go. Reverse direction and roll your head the other way. Take a deep breath and allow your neck and shoulders to relax.

Continue to move your attention upward toward your head and face. First, make a frown by wrinkling up your forehead as tightly as you can. Next, scrunch up your eyes, flare your nostrils, and clench your jaw. Finally, compress your lips into a tight circle. Pull your lips as tight as a miser's purse strings, hold it tighter and tighter, then relax and let go. Now, take a deep breath, relax your lips, and blow out forcefully.

Now mentally go back over the entire procedure, and feel the relaxation in your feet, ankles, calves, back, and chest. As you let go more and more, the relaxation deepens in your neck, shoulders, arms, and hands. Go deeper and deeper into being relaxed.

Finally, feel the relaxation extend to your head and face, your jaw hanging loose and your lips slightly parted.

If some tension persists in a specific part of your body, simply return your focus to that spot. Increase the tension, hold it, take a deep breath, and then relax and let go.

While we are on the subject of letting go, let me tell you about the Buddha Board I received as a gift. The Buddha Board is based on the

Zen concept of living in the moment. When you paint on the surface of the board with plain water, your image comes to life, and then, as the water evaporates, your artwork magically disappears, leaving you with a clean slate and a clear mind. What a lovely way to live!

And here is one more valuable tool you can add to your toolbox. It is called "relaxation visualization" or "relaxation imagery," and it is ideally used right after your progressive relaxation technique. Together they can be extremely powerful. The goal of this exercise is to be able to call up at a moment's notice, a peaceful, relaxing scene whenever you need to. Again, this is borrowed from the *Anger Control Workbook*.

Earlier in this guide, we learned a stress-management technique using visualization; this is similar, but it is designed to be used at a moment's notice, no matter where you are. The idea is to visualize in detail a time and place where you felt especially safe, secure, and perfectly at peace. This is one of a number of possible meditations.

You are walking down a path through the woods with many trees on the left and right. Eventually, you see a light at the end of the path, and you come to a meadow, a peaceful clearing where the sun is shining, warming your skin, and the grass smells lush. You can hear the tinkling of a brook nearby.

Perhaps it's just this meadow that you have been looking for, or maybe you'll want to continue down the road that leads to the beach, where the waves come and go, caressing the white sand. Here, the salty smell in the air clears your mind, and the sound of the waves lulls you into a peaceful, almost hypnotic state.

Or, perhaps you see in the distance a cottage tucked into the side of a hill, with smoke lazily rising from the chimney. Inside, it's cozy in front of the fireplace. The smell of your favorite soup wafts from the kitchen and permeates the air, bringing back warm, nurturing memories. It is a place of peace.

Other similar meditations are just as effective, and a number of guided meditation CDs are on the market. However, for maximum effectiveness, it might be best to create your own personal relaxation image. This can be quite effective. Perhaps one of the scenarios above triggered a memory for you. Or maybe a childhood scene, a time of innocence, will work for you.

Begin creating your scene slowly, with your eyes closed, sketching it in broad strokes like an artist preparing a major canvas. Visualize the scene, and then anchor it to a specific time and place. Now start to fill in the details, the shapes and colors, the quality of light and shadow.

Next, add the dimension of sound: blackbirds in the reeds along a secluded road or migrating geese as they fly overhead or waves washing up on a peaceful shore. Perhaps you can hear the faint melody of a long-forgotten tune.

Now, explore the tactile qualities of the place. Become aware of the temperature, whether the sun is warm on your skin or a pleasant, cool breeze is blowing. If you're lying on the grass, notice the tickling sensation of the blades brushing your ear when you turn your head.

And remember the unique smells—freshly mown grass, bread just out of the oven, honeysuckle on the vine . . .

Finally, pay attention to the emotional "feel." Become aware of ripples of calmness and the reassuring feeling of safety and security. A sense of peace and tranquility pervades the entire scene.

When you have finished creating this mental refuge of peace, stop for a minute and savor the experience. Drink it in, memorizing all the components. Let all the sights, sounds, smells, and feelings sink into your awareness. Now anchor the scene with a key word, such as "mountains" or "the beach."

Open your eyes and look around and notice where you are in the real world. Go back to the relaxation image. Use your key word. Allow yourself to become fully immersed in the scene. See it, hear it, feel it. Notice the accompanying sense of security, peace, and relaxation. Now come back to the room again.

In order to help you achieve the transition from the here-and-now to your relaxation scene as quickly as possible, it's sometimes useful to imagine a magic door. Science fiction fans will be familiar with this concept as "teleportation," in which you are literally transported from one place to another, instantly.

Face the nearest blank wall and picture a door with a brass knob and a brass plaque. The plaque has your key work inscribed on it. When you turn the knob and open the door, you find, to your surprise, that your relaxation scene is full blown there before you. All you need do is cross the threshold, and you are safe and secure. With a little practice, you will be able to cross this magic threshold and enter your relaxation scene any time you feel the need.

At times you may not even be aware of your lack of self-forgiveness, so it is wise, periodically, to check yourself out, body, mind, and spirit:

- Do you eat balanced meals that you can look forward to and enjoy? If not, then at least remember to take your vitamins.
- Do you take care of your grooming and hygiene? What about the clothes you wear? Are they flattering? Do they help you feel good about yourself?
- What kind of regular exercise program do you have? How about trying something new? If you have never practiced yoga, Pilates, or tai chi, consider taking a class. What about strength training? If that doesn't sound appealing, maybe resistance bands are your answer.
- Do you have regular contact with friends? Do you have a sense of belonging through membership in sports groups, hobby clubs, community activity groups, church, or educational groups?
- Do you make time to just have fun, and do you have regular contact with supportive and interested family members? Do you make certain you are generous with your time in giving and doing things with others?
- Do you feel you have a purpose in life? How about setting goals in alignment with that purpose?
- Have you established proper boundaries for yourself? Do you have the ability to say no to things you don't want to experience?

- Do you live in the present moment—instead of obsessing about the past or worrying about the future?
- Do you push yourself to the limit, demanding total perfection from yourself?
- Do you take sufficient time for relaxation, such as reading books, watching videos, going to plays, or going to movies?

As you think of things you can add to this list, realize that it's not enough to want to do something. You need to plan whatever it is and then integrate it into your life.

I once heard it suggested that we look at life as if it were a favorite recipe. For example, as I thought about all the ingredients I needed to collect for my mom's chocolate cake, I realized that if I tried to use only the sweet ingredients, my baking would be inedible. Just as a cake recipe calls for baking soda as well as butter and sugar, so too does life demand a certain amount of sour with the sweet. For complete and balanced lives, we actually need bitter experiences in the same way a cake needs all its ingredients to make it a good cake.

Similarly, we can't just toss everything into a pan and put it in the oven. We have to mix the ingredients and make sure to get rid of any lumps. Similarly, we have to work on "the lumps" and integrate the sweet and the bitter portions of our lives to be able to extract the wisdom to produce a great life.

Once we understand there is a bigger purpose for what goes on in life and begin to look for reasons for why a particular circumstance may have happened, we can begin to forgive ourselves.

Take time now to think about all the skills you have gained that will help you turn your life around. Hopefully, you have picked up some new techniques you can use to call up peaceful images and rediscovered ways to develop a positive attitude and change the way you view the events of your life.

In reviewing your journey toward self-forgiveness, recall the story you wrote early in the book. Can you see, from your perspective then, just how limiting it was? Now, looking back at that story, you will realize that when you met an obstacle on the road of life, yes, it hurt, but you are now back on the road and can talk about the present instead of the past. You can also talk about what's important to you, not what's important to everyone else.

Each one of us has different gifts, because we have had different experiences. Make a list of everything you have gained and learned from having experienced a particular incident in your life, and ask yourself, "What wisdom can I contribute to the world now that I could not have contributed before I had those particular circumstances in my history?"

Recognizing your personal gifts is a vital step in your journey toward self-forgiveness. Until you find the blessings inherent in negative events, they will continue to exert negative control over you and keep you from moving forward.

What are your personal gifts?

_____
_____
_____
_____
_____
_____
_____
_____
_____
_____
_____
_____
_____

Velma Callan Harland

Now rewrite your story.

It is important to learn to let go as you are forgiving yourself. A friend who was seeing a psychiatrist shared with me a technique she had been given as homework. She was told to schedule time each day for rethinking her perceived past mistakes. No longer than seven minutes. She was told to set a timer. When the timer rang, that was it, she was finished rehashing things. When unwanted thoughts came up during the rest of the day, she just told herself she would deal with it at her scheduled time tomorrow. As time went on she found that often she didn't need her scheduled time to rehash her past. She had moved on.

Another process I like to use is to make a list, with a water soluble pen, of everything that is bothering me. Write it all down and then put the paper in a sink filled with water and watch all your difficulties disappear. I like to add the words "shame", "guilt," and anything else I think of that I need to let go of. Now, just tell yourself it is gone, finished.

Next, write yourself a letter following this example:

Dear _____ (your name),

I can forgive myself for the decisions and choices I made in the past. I understand that no circumstance or event in my life is a failure as long as I learn from the experience, and I am so grateful for that realization.

I release judgment and self-condemnation so that I may continue to move forward toward my future without being chained to my past.

Love,
_____ (your name)

See yourself in your imagination taping this letter to helium-filled balloon. Release the balloon and watch as it rises and fades from view, and repeat, "I release and let go." If you find there is something you are having a hard time letting go of, repeat these exercises as often as needed as you work on forgiving yourself.

I suggest that you also find someone who you can talk to about your need for self-forgiveness. That person needs to be able to actively support you in the process of letting go. Sharing the things you feel most badly about with a loving, compassionate person will help you ease the burden of guilt, but it will not be easy to do. Telling the whole truth to another person can be a terrifying process, making you feel vulnerable and open to rejection. However, the fear of telling another person about shame, guilt, and pain is minimal compared to the relief and joy you will feel when you do it and find that you are still accepted by that person.

Sometimes, progress seems painfully slow. Sometimes, it might even seem like you are going backward instead of forward. Consider that perhaps this simply means you have changed, have developed, and are even more aware of what is going on inside your own head. That is real progress; it is not backsliding at all! Perhaps you have just begun to work at a deeper level or have just removed another layer of the onion. Accept that you will always be able to go deeper and find more to learn. It is the work of a lifetime—onions have many layers.

As we come to the end of our trip together, you need to have a plan for the days and months ahead—a plan for how you are going to use what you have learned along the way. A plan motivates us to continue our journey and encourages us to be accountable for our efforts, so it is essential that you set goals for yourself.

What Goes into a Good Plan?

Be *Specific*
Instead of, "I am going to get more exercise," make your goal: "I am going mall walking with the walking group every Tuesday and Thursday at 9 a.m."

Be Realistic
Instead of saying you are going to join a book club, take computer lessons, join a meditation group, and become the secretary for the PTA, pick one and follow through.

Be Creative
Think of something you have always wanted to do that could help you enjoy life more fully. It could be as simple as starting a gratitude journal, or it could be something more involved, such as joining a curling club.

My Plan
I make the following commitment to myself for my journey to self-forgiveness.

_____
_____
_____
_____
_____
_____
_____
_____
_____
_____
_____
_____
_____
_____
_____
_____
_____

Velma Callan Harland

To reduce stress, I will make the following specific changes in my daily routine.

_____
_____
_____
_____
_____
_____
_____
_____
_____
_____
_____
_____
_____
_____
_____
_____
_____
_____
_____
_____
_____
_____
_____
_____
_____

In order to enjoy life more thoroughly, I commit to this plan.

_____ *(your name)*

Date: _____

Please be sure to review your plan often. I do so every week, usually on Sundays.

It is hard to face the truth, and sometimes the truth can hurt. By thinking about what is really going on in your life, you have accomplished a very difficult thing.

While working through this guidebook, you have acquired the skills, tools, and talents to move forward toward your goal of self-forgiveness. You will become better at the process the more you use it and a stronger person at the same time.

Bon voyage!

Sources and Related Reading

Beattie, Melody. *Co-Dependent's Guide to the Twelve Steps:* New York: Simon & Schuster, 2004.

Borris-Dunchunstang, Eileen. *Finding Forgiveness: A 7-Step Program for Letting Go of Anger and Bitterness.* New York: McGraw-Hill, 2007.

Cameron, Julia. *The Artist's Way: A Spiritual Path to Higher Creativity.* New York: Tarcher/Putnam, 1992.

Cameron, Julia. *The Artist's Way Workbook.* New York: Tharcher/Penguin, 2006.

Emoto, Masaru. *The Hidden Messages in Water.* Oregon: Beyond Words Publishing, 2006.

Ford, Debbie. *Why Good People Do bad Things: How to Stop Being Your Own Worst Enemy.* New York: Harper One, 2008.

Luskin, Dr. Fred. *Forgive for Good: A Proven Prescription for Health and Happiness.* New York:

Mc Call, Peggy. *Your Destiny Switvh: Master Your Key Emotion and Attract the life of Your Dreams.* Hay House, 2007.

Mc Kay, Matthew and Rogers D. Peter. *The Anger Control Workbook.* Oakland, CA: New Harbinger Publications, Inc. 2000.

Reed, Gayle L. *Forgiveness: A New Story.* Also an Article in October 2006 issue of the Consulting and Clinical Psychology. (on research with emotionally abused women and forgiveness therapy.

Tolle, Eckhart. *A New Earth: Awakening to Your Life's Purpose.* New York: Plume Publishing, 2006.

About the Author

Velma Harland was educated in Christian ministries at St. John's College in Winnipeg, Manitoba, Canada. She graduated with a Certificate in Theology from the University of Winnipeg and also graduated with a certificate in Applied Counseling at the University of Manitoba.

Velma felt drawn into forgiveness work and studied with Dr. S. Simon, author and forgiveness workshop leader. She also trained with Dr. Fred Luskin, author of *Forgive for Good* and current director of the Stanford University Forgiveness Project.

At her own forgiveness workshops, Velma was regularly asked, "How do we go about forgiving ourselves?" That was the question that motivated her interest in writing this book.

Velma also compiled and co-authored *If Nothing Changes, Nothing Changes*, a book of stories about people affected by the addictions of others in their lives. It was published by the Addictions Foundation of Manitoba.

Velma became a yoga instructor in 1975 and still teaches, specializing in yoga for cancer survivors.

She and her husband have raised five sons.